ANCIENT CIVILIZATIONS

A DAY IN ANCIENT CHINA

by Janie Havemeyer
illustrated by Cesar Samaniego

Tools for Parents & Teachers

Grasshopper Books enhance imagination and introduce the earliest readers to fun storylines and illustrations. The easy-to-read text supports early reading experiences with repetitive sentence patterns and sight words.

Before Reading

- Discuss the cover illustration. What do readers see?

- Look at the glossary together. Discuss the words.

Read the Book

- Read the book to the child, or have them read independently.

- "Walk" through the book and look at the illustrations. When and where does the story take place? What is happening in the story?

After Reading

- Prompt the child to think more. Ask: What was life like in ancient China? What more would you like to learn about ancient China or the Tang Dynasty?

Grasshopper Books are published by Jump!
5357 Penn Avenue South
Minneapolis, MN 55419
www.jumplibrary.com

Copyright © 2025 Jump! International copyright reserved in all countries. No part of this book may be reproduced in any form without written permission from the publisher.

Library of Congress Cataloging-in-Publication Data

Names: Havemeyer, Janie, author.
Samaniego, César, 1975- illustrator.
Title: A day in ancient China / by Janie Havemeyer; illustrated by Cesar Samaniego.
Description: Minneapolis, MN: Jump!, Inc., [2025]
Series: Ancient civilizations | Includes index.
Audience: Ages 7-10
Identifiers: LCCN 2024020086 (print)
LCCN 2024020087 (ebook)
ISBN 9798892134743 (hardcover)
ISBN 9798892134750 (paperback)
ISBN 9798892134767 (ebook)
Subjects: LCSH: China–History–Tang dynasty, 618-907–Juvenile literature.
Classification: LCC DS749.3 .H387 2025 (print)
LCC DS749.3 (ebook)
DDC 951/.017–dc23/eng/20240503
LC record available at https://lccn.loc.gov/2024020086
LC ebook record available at https://lccn.loc.gov/2024020087

Editor: Alyssa Sorenson
Direction and Layout: Anna Peterson
Illustrator: Cesar Samaniego
Content Consultant: Nicholas Williams, PhD, Associate Professor of Chinese Literature, Arizona State University

Printed in the United States of America at Corporate Graphics in North Mankato, Minnesota.

Table of Contents

Lighting Lanterns	4
Ancient China Timeline	22
Map of Ancient China	23
To Learn More	23
Glossary	24
Index	24

Lighting Lanterns

It is spring in China. The year is 691. People in Chang'an wake up early. This is the **capital**. People sell food, **livestock**, and more at the market.

rice field

Farmers also start the day early. Most people in **ancient** China farm. They have livestock like pigs and chickens. Some grow wheat, barley, rice, and vegetables. These plants feed many people in the country.

Children are busy, too. Boys farm. Girls help their moms. They gather threads from silkworm cocoons. They twist the threads together. These will be used to make silk clothing.

In town, rich people live in large homes. Some spend time painting. Others write poems or play weiqi. In this game, players use white and black stones to take over areas on the board.

Girls watch their mothers and grandmothers. They learn how to run a home. Today, they are making sweet rice balls. These are for tonight's Lantern Festival! Everyone will celebrate.

People work hard in the city.
A villager sells firewood.
A baker sells pastries. People
decorate. They hang lanterns
for the festival. People watch
performers. They cheer and
toss them coins!

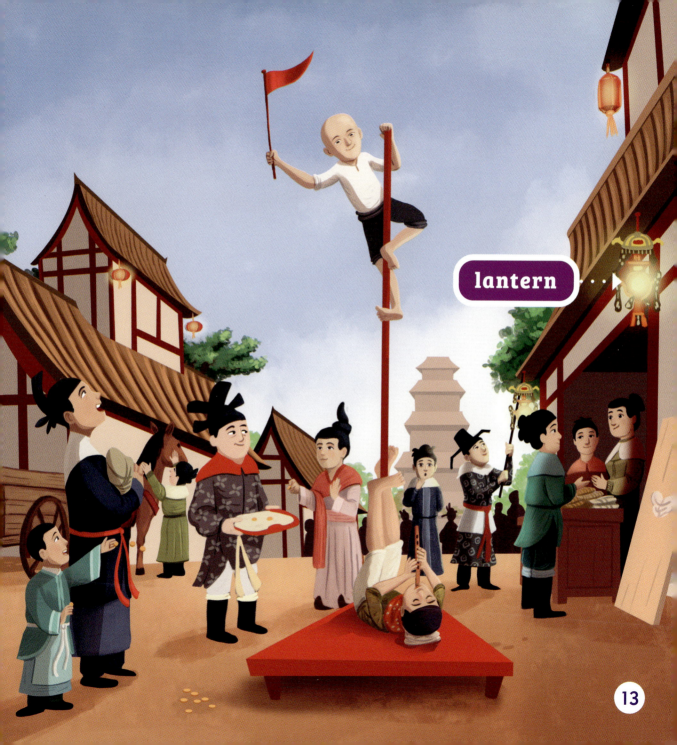

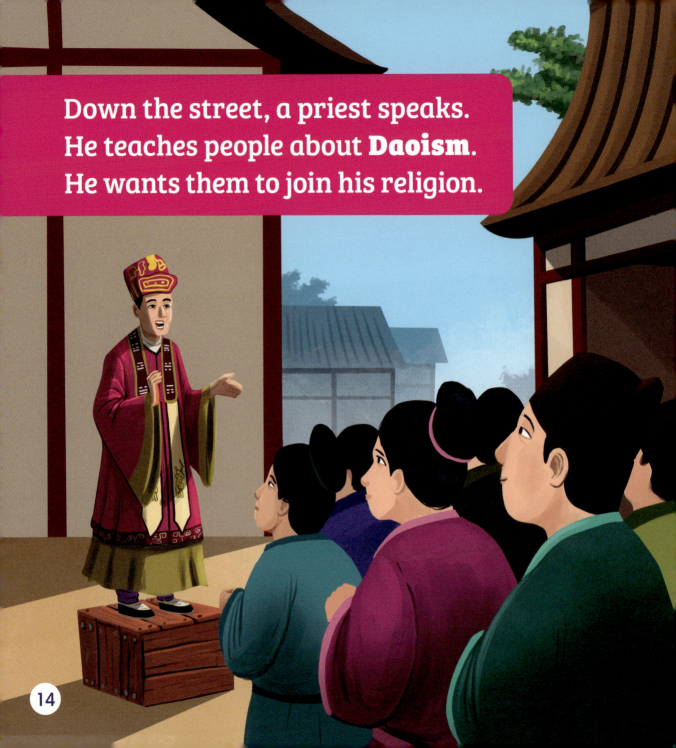

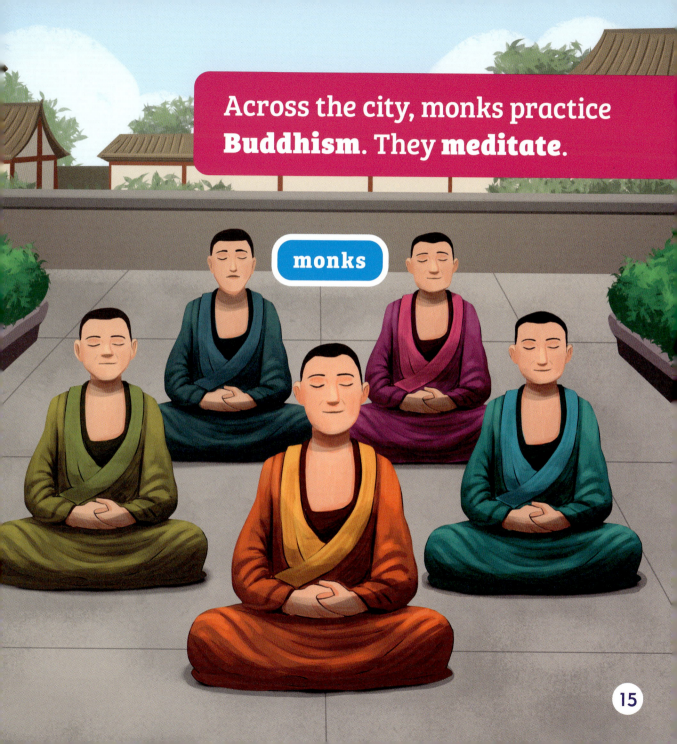

Wu Zetian loves art. She is the only **empress** to rule the country during the Tang **Dynasty**. She writes poetry. She invites poets to her palace in Chang'an. She reads their poems. She rewards the best!

At night, families gather. A grandmother makes dinner before the festival starts. There are dishes of fish, rice, and vegetables. Chopsticks click as everyone eats around a low table.

Then it is time for the Lantern Festival! It marks the new year's first full moon. Lanterns shine. People eat and dance. Firecrackers explode. Everyone comes together to celebrate!

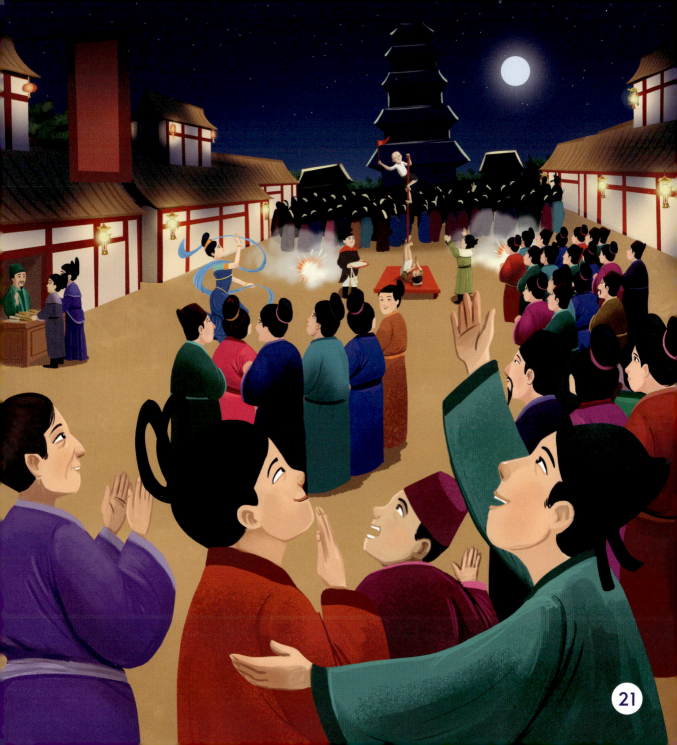

Ancient China Timeline

What are some important events in China's history? Take a look!

1046–256 BCE
The Zhou Dynasty is the longest-lasting dynasty.

221–206 BCE
The Qin Dynasty brings China together under one emperor. People start building what will later be the Great Wall of China.

105 CE
Paper is created.

581–618 CE
During the Sui Dynasty, the Grand Canal is built. It makes travel easier.

206 BCE–220 CE
During the Han Dynasty, a trade path called the Silk Road links China with western countries. Buddhism is brought to China.

618–907 CE
The Tang Dynasty is the golden age of ancient China. Wu Zetian is the first and only woman to rule the country. She rules from 690 to 705.

Map of Ancient China

Take a look at China during the Tang Dynasty.

To Learn More

Finding more information is as easy as 1, 2, 3.
❶ Go to www.factsurfer.com
❷ Enter "**ancientChina**" into the search box.
❸ Choose your book to see a list of websites.

Glossary

ancient: Very old or from the very distant past.

Buddhism: A way of life based on the teachings of the Buddha. Buddhists believe wanting is the cause of most suffering.

capital: The city in a country where the government is based.

Daoism: A religion that teaches how to live in harmony with the world.

dynasty: A line of rulers from the same family.

empress: A female ruler of an empire.

livestock: Animals that are kept or raised on a farm.

meditate: To think about something in a very focused way.

Index

Chang'an 4, 16

chopsticks 18

farm 5, 6

firecrackers 20

Lantern Festival 11, 12, 18, 20

livestock 4, 5

monks 15

performers 12

poems 8, 16

religion 14

rice 5, 11, 18

school 10

silk 6

Zetian, Wu 16